AF824067

13 ESSENTIAL LESSONS

FOR YOUTH AGES

14-18

Conversational, experiential lessons reveal how the Old Testament narrative points to Jesus' redemptive mission—and how these ancient truths impact teenagers' everyday lives.

No. 01

JESUS-CENTERED

100%

FROM THE

OLD TESTAMENT

13 Essential Lessons From the Old Testament

group.com
simplyyouthministry.com

Credits
Executive Developer: Tim Gilmour
Executive Editor: Rick Lawrence
Chief Creative Officer: Joani Schultz
Editor: Stephanie Martin
Art Director and Cover Art: Jeff Storm
Production: Suzi Jensen
Project Manager: Justin Boling

ISBN 978-1-4707-4289-8
10 9 8 7 6 5 4 3 2 1 21 20 19 18 17 16

Printed in the United States of America.

TABLE OF CONTENTS

- [X] EASILY REPRODUCIBLE
- [X] OPEN-ENDED QUESTIONS
- [X] FLEXIBLE FOR ANY SIZE GROUP
- [X] WRITTEN USING THE NEW LIVING TRANSLATION
- [X] ENGAGING ACTIVITIES

HOW TO USE THESE LESSONS...

This collection of *13 Essential Lessons From the Old Testament* is a taste-test overview of crucial topics, threaded through a narrative that is always pointing forward to the Messiah. The lessons are structured simply, using an "inquiry based" method that maximizes conversation and engagement with your teenagers. This question-focused structure gives you the flexibility to tailor these lessons to your time slot, and go as deep as your group is able to go. We believe healthy discussion is essential to help students own their faith. Even more, you don't have to be a theologian to lead these lessons. We've crafted them specifically to emphasize discussion and deeper connections among students. If you love God and love teenagers, you can easily lead these lessons.

Each lesson is built on Group's REAL teaching imperatives: Relational, Experiential, Applicable, and Learner-based. Each week, your kids will build relationships with each other, and with God, through interactive experiences and challenging questions that will spur them to dig deeper. And every lesson is threaded-through with a Jesus-centered focus that reveals and elevates the Messiah, no matter what the topic or scriptural foundation. In addition, we include ideas for connecting what kids are learning to their everyday lives with every lesson. The lecture (or "talk") strategy that so many use as a default setting has proven to be the least effective way for people—not just teenagers—to learn. In fact, more and more learning experts are now branding the talking-at-you method so popular in churches as "educational malpractice." With these lessons, you get a "best practice" approach that will plant growth in your students.

As an added resource, we've included a short "background" segment that will help you quickly get up to speed on the topic focus of each lesson. And we've included two suggested "Tweet-able" invitations you can send out to teenagers in advance of each lesson.

Now, just like that, you're ready to lead these lessons. Follow the flow from start to finish, or cherry-pick the lessons that fit your scope. We're so grateful you've picked up this resource, and honored to partner with you in your ministry to teenagers.

Grace,

Rick Lawrence
Editorial Director
Group/Simply Youth Ministry Resources

LESSON No.01

GOD IS HOLY

BIBLE VERSES

Isaiah 6:1-5 John 12:25-26
Romans 12:1 1 Peter 1:16

ACTIVITY

Ask: **How would you define the word "holy," and why?**

After students answer that question, grab the supplies and cut open both pieces of chocolate.

Ask: **Which of these is the better illustration for what holiness is all about, and why?**

Say: **Holiness means you're without blemish or sin; in other words, you're pure. What you see on the outside is what's on the inside. You're the same all the way through. With the solid piece of chocolate, you can see that it's the same on the inside and the outside. It's complete and whole, all the way through. With the candy bar, you can see that the outside is covered in chocolate, but the inside is something different. When we talk about God's holiness, we're talking about this solid piece of chocolate: God is the same, complete and whole, all the way through.**

Things you need...

- ☐ Bibles
- ☐ A solid piece of chocolate
- ☐ A chocolate-covered candy bar
- ☐ A sharp knife

DIGGING IN

Have someone read aloud Isaiah 6:1-5.

Say: **Let's spend some time talking about the holiness of God.**

ACKNOWLEDGE THAT YOU NEED GOD

Say: **It might seem a little scary or intimidating to consider exactly how holy God is. But a deeper understanding of what "holy" really means can create a sense of wonder and a magnetic attraction to God, not a fear that he'll strike us down or punish us. Even though we're in a kind of prison because of our sin, we can be set free by Jesus when we acknowledge our need for him, and our need for forgiveness. When this happens, the sins that separate us from God are resolved by Jesus' sacrifice on the cross, and we can be in God's presence without fear.**

BIBLE BACKGROUND

Read Isaiah 6:1-5.

A basic fundamental of the Christian faith is God's holiness. God is a perfect Creator who is without sin. God's holiness reveals our brokenness, showing us our need for a Savior. There are no shadows on the sun's surface, and there can be no sin in God's presence. However, we can stand in God's presence through the saving work of Jesus.

The prophet Isaiah receives a vision of what God looks like. He sees the incredible majesty and splendor of God's throne. In this Bible passage, we see that even the seraphim are unable to look at God because of his complete holiness. They fly around with their eyes covered. They're also constantly declaring how holy God is. It's as if God's holiness is so consuming, it's all you can think about when you're in his presence. When Isaiah sees this vision, he realizes how unworthy he really is in the presence of such a holy God.

Ask:

- **Why do you think Isaiah was given this vision of God in heaven?**
- **When you read these verses from Isaiah, do you feel more or less able to actually relate to God? Explain.**
- **Why do you think Isaiah said he was doomed after he saw this vision?**
- **When have you felt both close to and far away from God? Explain.**

BECOME MORE LIKE JESUS

Say: **Jesus, who's perfect and without sin, gives us strength to overcome things in this life that pull us away from him. As we grow spiritually, getting to know Jesus more deeply and therefore becoming more like him, our thoughts and actions start to reflect the thoughts and actions of God, who is holy. Your inside starts to look more like your outside, and vice-versa.**

Ask:

- **As you've gotten to know Jesus, what's one way you've actually become more like him? What impact has this area of growth had on your overall life?**
- **What's one area where you want to grow but seem to be struggling to become more like Jesus? Why do you think it's such a struggle?**

CONTINUE TO WALK WITH GOD

Say: **Jesus wants all people to be in heaven with him for eternity. But he lets us choose whether we'll follow him and how we'll live. Jesus desires for us to continue walking with him throughout our lives. This means dying to self and becoming more complete as we mature spiritually.**

Have someone read aloud John 12:25-26.

Ask: **How can you practice these words from Jesus in your daily life?**

DIGGING DEEPER

Ask:

- **Holiness can be a tough concept to fully understand. Why do you think holiness is one of God's characteristics? What would happen to us if God weren't holy?**
- **Read 1 Peter 1:16. Why does God want you to be holy? If you think about holiness as working hard to be perfect, that seems hopeless. Why would God tell us to do something that seems impossible in our own strength?**

Say: **Jesus wants his followers to live holy lives. This doesn't mean being perfect, but allowing his work in our lives to make us more like him—more complete, inside and out.**

PUTTING IT INTO PRACTICE

Ask:

- **What are some first steps you can take to make yourself more open to Jesus developing holiness in you?**
- **Read Romans 12:1. This verse says there's a connection between living holy and worshiping Jesus. Pause for a moment and meditate silently on this verse. Why is there a connection between holiness and worship?**
- **How have you felt encouraged by someone to live a holy life? What are some practical steps you can take to do the same for someone else?**

THINGS TO REMEMBER

TEXTS & TWEETS

How do you define holiness? Let's talk about it in real ways. Can't wait to see you!

Yep, you can be holy the way God is holy. Get ready to dig deep, and bring a friend.

Make texting your group easier. Consider using Simply Text. To try it FREE go to https://secure.symt.us/signup

LESSON No.02

GOD IS JUST

BIBLE VERSES

Psalm 99:4 Psalm 7:17 Psalm 11:4-7 John 3:16-18
Psalm 92:12-15 Isaiah 1:16-17 Isaiah: 61:8-9

ACTIVITY

Say: **Let's start off with a surprise. I didn't tell you ahead of time, but I decided to bring along some food. Let's dig into some pie** [pizza or snack] **before we get started!**

Once students see the food, they'll likely compete for the largest slices. That's fine. Let each person eat a slice.

Ask:

- **Who got the biggest piece? Did you consider offering it to someone else in the group first? Why or why not?**
- **Who got the smallest slice? Why did you end up with it?**
- **Was this experience fair or just? Why or why not?**

Say: **Today we'll talk about one of God's characteristics that fits right in with our food experience. God is just. He sees and treats everyone the same. God doesn't care if you're an athlete, cheerleader, Chess Club president, band member, top of your class, or bottom of your class. God judges and views everyone with the same level of wisdom, love, and passion.**

Things you need...

- ☐ Bibles
- ☐ An inexpensive pie or pizza or large snack cut into pieces of *varying* sizes, with one piece for every student

DIGGING IN

Have someone read aloud Psalm 99:4.

Say: **Let's spend a few moments looking at how just God is.**

GOD LOVES JUSTICE

Have someone read aloud Isaiah 61:8-9 and Psalm 11:4-7.

Ask:

- **Why does God have such a love for justice?**
- **What would our lives be like if God weren't just?**
- **Psalm 11:5-6 offers some harsh words about God's attitude toward people who love violence and are unjust toward others. If God is so opposed to injustice, why is it still so prevalent?**

BIBLE BACKGROUND

Read Psalm 99:4.

This verse describes God as a "lover of justice" who has "acted with justice and righteousness" in his relationship with Israel. When we talk about God being "just," we mean he acts in a righteous manner and desires a right relationship with his people. Being just also means us having a right relationship with other people.

Encourage students to think about their relationship with God and their relationships with other people. Are those relationships defined by righteousness—right acts, right motives, and right attitudes? When those things are absent, we experience injustice, which God hates and wants us to confront in our world.

There is a right and a wrong. God is consistent and doesn't flip-flop back and forth at random. He hates the evil that happens in the world, and one day he'll settle all accounts. As Christians, we can choose to pursue and love justice—not what's easy or convenient or expedient.

- **What do you think it means to experience a just, right relationship with God? What's it like to have that kind of relationship with other people?**

Say: **God loves justice because he's pure. Being just means having a very clear sense of right and wrong. If we're just, it means we're having right relationship with God and others. Justice is the foundation. There's a right and wrong. God is consistent and doesn't flip-flop back and forth at random. He hates the evil that happens in the world, and one day all accounts will be settled. As Christians, we can choose to pursue and love justice, not what's easy, convenient, or expedient.**

GOD HATES INJUSTICE

Say: **Growing closer to Jesus means becoming more like him. As our relationship with Jesus deepens, we start to gain a better understanding of justice. We have a greater awareness of injustice in the world, and we look for ways to address it. That's an important truth: Yes, Jesus wants us to recognize injustice, but he also calls us to act and respond when we see injustice being inflicted on other people.**

Ask:

- **What are some of the greatest injustices in the world right now? Why do you define them as unjust?**
- **How are these injustices affecting relationships?**
- **When you think about the people committing these injustices, what is likely true about their perspective of God?**
- **How has the world become either more just or less just than it was when Jesus walked the earth?**

DIGGING DEEPER

Ask:

- **Do you believe God holds you to the same level of accountability to act justly as a 70-year-old adult who's been a Christian for decades? Why or why not?**
- **Read Psalm 92:12-15. These Bible verses tell us that as godly people grow older, they'll continue to recognize that God is just. Why might this characteristic become clearer or more certain to you as get older?**
- **Look at verse 13. Why do you think godly people "flourish in the courts of our God"?**
- **Read Psalm 7:17. What are some experiences that have caused you to think of God's justice as a reason to give thanks and sing praises?**

- **Read John 3:16-18. How do these verses highlight the truths of justice and mercy that we've been discussing?**

PUTTING IT INTO PRACTICE

Ask:

- **Read Isaiah 1:16-17. What are some injustices that happen regularly at your school or among teenagers in our community?**
- **As a young person, what are some ways you have already pursued justice in your everyday life? If you're interested in working for justice, how do you know what to pursue?**
- **Each of us deserves to spend eternity separated from God, but because of Jesus' death and resurrection, we have the opportunity to receive God's mercy and forgiveness. What's one way you've shown a merciful attitude toward someone in your life?**

THINGS TO REMEMBER

TEXTS & TWEETS

God is just, but what impact does that have on your life? Join us for a great discussion.

Are you getting what you deserve? Should you? See you soon!

13 ESSENTIAL LESSONS FROM THE OLD TESTAMENT

LESSON No.03

GOD IS PATIENT

BIBLE VERSES

Psalm 103
Nehemiah 9:30
1 Timothy 1:16
2 Peter 3:15

ACTIVITY

Say: **Learning patience isn't easy, especially when we're eager to take a new step or receive something new. In this scene from *Star Wars: The Empire Strikes Back*, we'll see how Luke struggles to be patient with an odd character. Luke is impatient about meeting Yoda, the Jedi Master, but Luke doesn't realize he's already talking to Yoda, the very one he's seeking.**

Play the clip.

Ask:

- **Why is Luke so impatient?**
- **How does Luke's impatience blind him in this situation?**
- **What's a recent example of how impatience blinded you, and what were the consequences of your impatience? What did you learn from that situation?**

DIGGING IN

Have students take turns reading aloud Psalm 103.

Say: **Let's spend a few moments talking about God's patience.**

GOD IS PATIENT AND WANTS US TO RETURN TO HIM

Say: **God's character is revealed through actions. He demonstrates love by waiting on us and allowing us to recognize our need for forgiveness. God wants us to understand that even though we don't deserve it, we have the opportunity, through Jesus' death and resurrection, to seek and receive forgiveness.**

Ask:

- **The psalmist reminds us in Psalm 103:12 that when we seek forgiveness, God removes our sins as far as the east is from the west. Why is that sometimes hard to believe? Is the problem more about a lack of trust in God, or a lack of trust in yourself?**

Things you need...

- ☐ Bibles
- ☐ A video clip from *Star Wars: The Empire Strikes Back*, from 0:54:00, as Luke sits inside Yoda's home, to 0:57:00, as Luke pleads with Yoda
- ☐ An Internet connection and a computer or tablet to display the video

BIBLE BACKGROUND

Read Psalm 103.

This incredible psalm, attributed to David, reflects a deep understanding of God's character. He patiently waits on us to seek forgiveness and a restored relationship. Verse 8 reveals God's patience; he's slow to get angry. In verse 10, we discover that love causes God to hold off punishment for the sins we commit. Verses 15-16 remind us we won't live forever. We must make a choice to receive God's forgiveness and follow Christ while we still have the chance.

- **The story of Israel in the Old Testament includes several experiences when God instructed the people to make memorials to remember past events. What are some "markers" in your life—something that reminds you of God's love for you?**

GOD WANTS US TO BE PATIENT LIKE HE IS

Ask:

- **Is patience just something some people are born with, or can you learn to be patient? Explain. What's involved in learning to be patient, and how is Jesus involved in that process?**
- **Looking at your own life, do you believe Jesus is slow to get and stay angry with you? Why or why not?**
- **How much do you reflect that same characteristic to others around you? Are you slow to get angry with people who hurt or offend you? Why or why not?**
- **How has patience helped you grow in your relationship with God?**

Say: **Developing patience helps us gain a more Christ-like perspective about what matters most in life, and it helps us grow in our trust and faith in Jesus. We want things to happen right now, but that isn't always how God plans things. Patience opens the door to a deeper experience in our relationship with Jesus.**

DIGGING DEEPER

Ask:

- **Psalm 103 reminds us that life is fragile. Teenagers can often feel as if they're unstoppable—that their whole life is in front of them. Although this seems true, none of us has a guarantee on how long our life will be. How does this truth impact your choices and the way you live right now, if at all?**
- **Read verse 16. The psalmist says that after you've died, it will seem as though you'd never been here. How does that truth affect your perspective on the way you live your life? Are your priorities consistent with what Jesus desires? Why or why not?**
- **Read Nehemiah 9:30. Why would God display such patience with the Israelites, who were repeatedly disobedient and rebellious?**
- **Read 2 Peter 3:15. God is willing to wait for people to respond to the gift of forgiveness made available through Jesus. Why do you think he's willing to wait for humanity to seek forgiveness instead of simply forcing us to repent? How does this verse affect your attitude toward those who don't follow Jesus?**

DIGGING DEEPER

Ask:

- **Take a moment to silently reflect. What are some ways you've seen Jesus' patience lived out in your life?**
- **People often want to get back at those who treat them wrong or hurt them. Yet Jesus shows a willingness to forgive—over and over again. What is easy and difficult about forgiving others?**

PUTTING IT INTO PRACTICE

Ask:

- **The writer of Psalm 103 clearly is excited because of what God has done in his life. He says he'll never forget what God has done for him. What are some things God has done in your life recently that you don't want to forget?**
- **Read 1 Timothy 1:16. Paul says people can look at his life to see Jesus' patience. How has Jesus moved through other people's lives to help you grow? What patient person is one of your role models, and why?**

THINGS TO REMEMBER

TEXTS & TWEETS

Got patience? Does God? Let's explore how to grow in patience together.

Are you struggling to be patient? Come discover where to find help.

Make texting your group easier. Consider using Simply Text. To try it FREE go to https://secure.symt.us/signup

LESSON No.04

GOD IS LOVING

BIBLE VERSES

Psalm 144 John 3:16
Jeremiah 31:3 1 John 4:7-10, 19

ACTIVITY

Say: **I've brought in something that reflects what love is all about. It's a reflection of someone's love for me, and I've kept it because of my love for this person. It isn't valuable to anyone else, but it means the world to me because of the person who gave it to me.**

Display the item and explain its significance to you.

Ask: **What do you have with you right now that reminds you of how someone in your life loves you?** (Pause as a few teenagers share)

Say: **Let's look at God's love for humanity—at how much God loves you and me. God's love is so much deeper and stronger than the love we can feel toward another person, and it was displayed most passionately through the gift of Jesus, God's Son.**

Things you need...

- ☐ Bibles
- ☐ Something simple you were given that means a lot to you (a card from a loved one, an art project from a child, etc.)

DIGGING IN

Have students take turns reading aloud Psalm 144.

Say: **Let's spend some time talking about God's love for us.**

GOD LOVED US ENOUGH TO CREATE US

Ask:

- **How have you experienced God's love in your life? What does his love mean to you personally? Be as specific and personal as you can.**
- **In Psalm 144, where do you see evidence of God's love? What are some of his character traits or actions that display his love?**
- **Have you ever had moments in your life when you felt unwanted? If so, what created those feelings, and how did you handle the experience?**

Say: **You're not an accident—you're wanted. There isn't a single "accidental" person here on earth. There never has been and never**

BIBLE BACKGROUND

Read Psalm 144.

God's love is amazing—it's beyond understanding! God's love for us isn't conditional, meaning it isn't based on our faithfulness or anything we do. We can't be good enough to earn it, and we can't be bad enough to lose it. Throughout the Bible, from Genesis to Revelation, we discover the story of a Creator who loves humanity enough to protect us from harm and provide for our needs. He chooses to do this; no one forces him!

The word "love" is used a ton in our world: We love our families, and we love a favorite food or band. As you and your students explore God's loving nature, work to gain a specific, personal understanding of God's love.

will be. God has a passion and a vision for everyone who has ever lived or will ever live. That vision is for us to spend eternity with him, starting right now, if we'll ask for God's forgiveness and follow Jesus. This invitation is for everyone, regardless of where you come from or who you are. God's vision for your life also includes discovering how you can live in a way that honors Jesus, who created you and loves you.

GOD'S LOVE PROTECTS

Ask:

- **What's the importance of the psalmist reminding you that God is your protector? God doesn't physically walk next to you at school or in your neighborhood, so how can this truth about God as your protector help you live out your faith?**
- **Think back to your early childhood, when a parent or some other adult kept you safe in a dangerous situation. How did you feel? How has the intensity of your feeling of safety and security changed as you've gotten older?**

Say: **It isn't always easy—in fact, it's often difficult—but a life spent following Jesus means we're learning to depend on him to protect us. God wants to be the one we go to when we have a need or feel scared about something. He wants to protect us in the same way earthly parents protect their children.**

GOD'S LOVE PROVIDES

Ask:

- **Do you keep track of your prayer requests and how Jesus answers them? Why or why not? If you do keep track, how has that affected your spiritual growth?**
- **The psalmist reminds us of how much God wants to provide for us—a desire motivated by his love. What are some ways God has provided for you in the last week, month, and year? What can you learn from these examples of provision?**

Say: **God promises to provide for us and meet our needs. He doesn't promise wealth, popularity, or fame, but he does promise to take care of our needs and bless our lives. And because of these blessings, people will know that our faith is alive and Jesus is true and living.**

DIGGING DEEPER

Ask:

- **Psalm 144:3-4 reminds us how small and frail humanity is** compared to God. What typically makes you feel small and frail, and how do you cope with those feelings?

- Even though we don't deserve it because of our sins, God still loves us. We can experience forgiveness when we first choose to follow Jesus, but we continue to need forgiveness when we stumble, struggle, and sin. And Jesus continues to love us. Does this surprise you on any level? Doesn't it seem as if Jesus would eventually give up on us and say we can't receive any more love or forgiveness? Explain.
- Read Jeremiah 31:3. God's love is limitless and without timeframes or conditions. How is this different from what our culture models or teaches about love?
- Jesus' love for humanity is amazing. Often people put limits on love, but Jesus' love is unconditional. Read John 3:16. Jesus' love is available to anyone who believes in him. It isn't limited by anything. In what ways is our love typically limited?
- When have you experienced unconditional love, and how did it impact you?

PUTTING IT INTO PRACTICE

- Read 1 John 4:7-10. These verses talk about how God is love and offer a description of what real love looks like. In your own words, how would you share these verses with a friend who isn't a Christian? How might this help your friend understand or experience Jesus' love?
- When have you experienced others loving you the way Jesus loves you? When have you loved others the way Jesus loves them?
- It can be hard to love others. God's Word, however, reminds us in 1 John 4:19 that we can love others because God loved us first. What people are you struggling to love right now, and why?
- What do you think it will take to get to the place where you can love these individuals? How have you learned to love people who you don't want to love? How has a person in your life helped you grow in your ability to love others?
- Why is it sometimes hard to love others? During the next week, what's one thing you can do to challenge and encourage someone in this area?

TEXTS & TWEETS

How loving are you? Do you love like Jesus does? See you soon for a love-ly discussion.

Need a little love? We have plenty to offer—and so does Jesus. Join us, and bring a friend!

Make texting your group easier. Consider using Simply Text. To try it FREE go to https://secure.symt.us/signup

THINGS TO REMEMBER

LESSON FAITH IN ACTION

No.05

BIBLE VERSES **Joshua 2:1-21** Joshua 6:17, 22-25 Matthew 1:5 Hebrews 11:3 James 2:25

ACTIVITY

Ahead of time, recruit a young child (grade 1-3) to simply stand alone near the entrance of your meeting room. If necessary, a parent of the child can be nearby but unseen. The goal is to have this child simply stand there—notice if anyone stops to help him or her. If anyone does, coach the child to simply say: **"Thanks, I'm waiting for my mom/dad here." When your meeting is ready to begin, bring the child in with you to stand next to you during your intro.**

Say: **This is ___________. I asked him/her to stand outside of our door before we got started, because I was curious to see how you interacted with him/her as you came into our gathering. I know that Jesus is always willing to move through my life to serve others, for his glory—as long as I'm available and recognize the opportunities. If I'm too busy, or in a rush, or distracted, I might miss windows of opportunity to make a difference.** (Here, ask the child if anyone stopped to help or say hello, then praise the group if that happened. If it didn't happen, don't say anything. Thank the child and have a parent take him/her away.) **If I'm too focused on my own needs, I might not be sensitive enough to notice when Jesus is leading me to focus on others. And if I'm not asking him for opportunities to serve others, I'll likely have fewer chances to help people in need.**

Ask:

- **When have you felt too busy, too discouraged, or too self-focused and missed an opportunity to serve others? Tell us about that experience.**
- **How and why have you struggled to understand and respond to Jesus' leading in your life?**
- **How have you overcome those struggles—or how have you attempted to overcome them?**

Things you need...

☐ Bibles

BIBLE BACKGROUND

Read Joshua 2:1-21; 6:17, 22-25.

Rahab is an unlikely heroine. A prostitute in the city of Jericho, she becomes a hero of the faith by believing that the God of Israel is real and by taking action to help God's cause. From inside the city, Rahab gives shelter and information to spies Joshua sends into the Promised Land.

Rahab puts her life in danger by deceiving the authorities who come to arrest Joshua's spies at her house. This story is full of intrigue and daring, with Rahab trusting God to spare her from destruction. And when the walls crumble, she and her family are saved.

In response to faith, God transforms the imperfect and makes insiders out of outsiders, turning them into faith heroes.

DIGGING IN

Have students take turns reading aloud Joshua 2:1-21; 6:17, 22-25.

Say: **This week's lesson gives us the chance to see how an Old Testament hero from the Bible—a woman named Rahab—recognized when God was at work. She responded and had the chance to make a big difference for God.**

HEAR THE MESSAGE

Ask:

- **Rahab's conversation in Joshua 2:9-11 with the spies, as they hid under the flax drying on her roof, reveals what she knows about God—"the supreme God of the heavens above and the earth below." How do you think Rahab had heard all these stories about God, and why is that significant?**
- **Why it is important for us to remember what God has done in the past—in our lives and in the lives of people who followed God in earlier generations?**

Say: **Rahab's faith in the God of the Israelites came from hearing about what he'd done to save his people 40 years before and how God continued keeping his promises to them. She isn't a Jew, but she believes in the one true God, and that he can be trusted, based on what she's heard from other people. Remember, social media, the Internet, and text messages weren't available to spread news back then. The stories of God's power spread from person to person, city to city, nation to nation.**

JOIN THE CAUSE

Say: **Rahab's profession makes her house a logical place for the spies to go to look for information and cover. But the spies probably don't expect her to join in the mission by giving them critical information, protecting them from the authorities, and helping them escape.**

Ask:

- **Why do some people join causes while others never do?**
- **What are some reasons Rahab's choice to risk her life on behalf of the spies is so surprising? What, if any, are God's prerequisites for moving through us to impact others?**
- **Respond to this statement: God loves us so much that he accepts us just the way we are, but God also loves us so much that he won't let us stay the way we are.**

ACT ON THE OPPORTUNITY

Say: **Rahab makes sure to talk about her belief in God while the spies are still there. She believes that God is strong and his promises are good, and she wants to be part of what God is doing. Because of Rahab's confession and her actions, the spies promise on behalf of Joshua that she and her family will be saved—and they are.**

Ask:

- **When was the last time you acted on a "nudge" from God and did something on his behalf?**
- **What are the typical obstacles you face in putting your faith into action?**

DIGGING DEEPER

Ask:

- **After escaping the destruction of Jericho, Rahab remains with the Israelites as a convert to faith in God, and even as an imperfect outsider she becomes a hero among the people for what she's done. Rahab is even mentioned in the New Testament as a reminder for us to act on our faith.** (See Matthew 1:5; Hebrews 11:31; and James 2:25.) **Who are some ordinary people you know or have heard about whose faith inspires you, and why?**
- **Rahab was faithful (Hebrews 11:31) and righteous (James 2:25); therefore, her life is an example worth following. Rahab acted in her best interests—she wanted her family to survive the Israelite invasion. Is this contradictory to being faithful and righteous? Explain why you feel that way.**

TEXTS & TWEETS

What's keeping you from living your faith? Don't miss our discussion about a surprising faith hero.

Don't feel ready to serve others? You may be more ready than you think. Find out this week, and be sure to invite a friend.

Make texting your group easier. Consider using Simply Text. To try it FREE go to https://secure.symt.us/signup

PUTTING IT INTO PRACTICE

- **One key to Rahab's faith is hearing and believing what God has done for his people. What is something God has done—either in the Bible or in your own life—that has helped your faith grow? Why did this experience or story have such an impact on your life?**
- **Where do you sense Jesus' influence in your life? What's one challenge he's asking you to take on or an opportunity he wants you to seize? What action steps can you take this week?**
- **Overall, how are you doing at putting your faith into action? How can you continue growing in this area?**

THINGS TO REMEMBER

LESSON No.06

HOPE RUNS IN THE FAMILY

BIBLE VERSES **Ruth 1:1-18** Ruth 4:9-22 Ruth 2:1-13

ACTIVITY

Welcome students and open in prayer.

Play the video clip.

Say: **The concept behind "random acts of kindness" is pretty simple: perform good deeds for strangers for no reason besides being kind. You're not asking for any money or thanks in return, and you may never see that person again. A little action can have a big impact, though, and can even start a domino effect of kindness.**

Ask:

- **What motivates people to perform random acts of kindness for strangers? What's easy or difficult about doing this? Explain.**
- **Have you ever done anything like this? What was it like, and how did people react?**
- **What's it like to have someone—either a stranger or someone you know—perform an act of kindness for you?**
- **Why do acts of kindness create hope in other people?**

Say: **You never really know when an act of kindness will make a big difference in someone's life. Maybe your small action will open the door for a conversation about Jesus, or maybe it will be a miraculous answer to a stranger's prayer. But an even better decision is pursuing a lifestyle of intentional kindness—not just random kindness—toward the people in your world. Each day can bring new opportunities for you to display the kindness, love, compassion, and grace Jesus has already shown you and asks you to show others.**

DIGGING IN

Have students read aloud Ruth 1:1-18; 2:1-13; 4:9-22.

Say: **Let's take a few minutes to see what we can discover from the incredible story of Ruth.**

Things you need...

- ☐ Bibles
- ☐ A video clip about random acts of kindness; for example, here's one about a high school student who started a kindness club at her high school: http://tinyurl.com/hv9cnpu
- ☐ An Internet connection and a computer or tablet to display the video

BIBLE BACKGROUND

Read Ruth 1:1-18; 2:1-13; 4:9-22.

Ruth is a native of Moab, a country (located in modern-day Jordan) that was often in conflict with its Israelite neighbors. Elimelech, his wife Naomi, and their family had left Bethlehem and moved to Moab to escape a famine. But then Elimelech and his sons, one of whom was Ruth's husband, all died, leaving the women to survive on their own in a time when unmarried women faced extraordinarily difficult circumstances if they didn't have family nearby.

When offered the chance to return to her own family for help, Ruth refuses and chooses to stay with her mother-in-law Naomi. This decision of faith and incredible devotion takes Ruth and Naomi back to Bethlehem, placing Ruth in a key position in God's plan. Boaz notices her character and work ethic. He ensures she'll be protected from harm and that she and Naomi won't go hungry. In the end, he marries Ruth, and their child is born into the lineage of David—which eventually leads to Jesus.

A HOPELESS PEOPLE

Say: **Naomi represents the people of Israel, who'd been living in exile and apart from God. She's the saddest and poorest of the Hebrews, dependent on an enemy for help. She's a reminder that we need reconciliation with God to truly experience hope in our lives.**

Ask:

- **What are some reasons people get trapped in hopelessness?**
- **When you feel distant from Jesus or separated from his love for you, how do you respond to what you're feeling inside? What do you do to try to resolve those feelings?**

A FAMILY BY FAITH

Ask:

- **Based on the Bible passages we read, what are some words that describe Ruth's attitude?**
- **How is Ruth's decision to go with Naomi similar to and different from our decision to follow Jesus?**

Say: **God's redemptive work in Ruth's life reminds us that he responds to those who trust him by making salvation available to all people, not just the Hebrews to whom he first revealed himself. Ruth is a determined, hard-working, grateful, loving woman. She's a Gentile who chooses to make Naomi's people her people and Naomi's God her God. By the same faith and choice, we're included in God's family.**

A REDEEMER BY DESIGN

Say: **Boaz's action is a preview of Jesus' willing act of redemption. When Elimelech's closer relative refuses to redeem his widow in chapter 4, Boaz willingly steps into the role of redeemer of Naomi, Ruth, and the family property. His redemptive act reminds us how Jesus willingly took our place on the cross and died for our sins.**

Ask:

- **What Boaz did wasn't really a random act of kindness, but it certainly had a significant impact on Ruth and her family. Do you think Ruth felt love for Boaz or merely an obligation to "pay him back" for his generosity? Explain.**
- **How is the story of Ruth and Boaz different from most modern-day love stories? What's significant about those differences?**
- **Jesus loves us on purpose, not randomly. How have you seen Jesus' specific and intentional love for you?**

DIGGING DEEPER

Ask:

- **Ruth is a foreigner, even an enemy of God's chosen people—making this a story of God's love for all people, not just the Jews. Ruth is poor, and though she willingly works hard, she depends on the kindness of others for her support. She's devoted to both God and Naomi, for which God blesses her. What else in the story of Ruth captures your attention?**
- **Ruth's declaration of faith and love is stunning in its beauty and simplicity. It's sometimes read at weddings, though it was originally spoken by a woman to her mother-in-law. What hints of Jesus' relationship with his bride—the church—do you see in this story?**

PUTTING IT INTO PRACTICE

Ask:

- **Many kids at your school struggle with feelings of hopelessness, isolation, or despair. What have you done in the past to come alongside people facing these feelings? What do these people need most, and how can they get it?**
- **Ruth made a bold declaration of commitment to Naomi, to her Hebrew family, and to God—and she stuck to it even when it was hard. When have you had a difficult time maintaining your commitment to loving God and other people? When have you recently doubted your relationship with Jesus or felt like giving up? Why didn't you? Or if you did, how are you working through your struggle?**
- **How have friends and others helped you stick to your commitments even when it's tough? What situations or circumstances can we pray about right now?**
- **Boaz's actions toward Ruth were motivated by love and compassion. What are some examples of how love and compassion are helping to guide your actions? What's one risk you can take, motivated by love and compassion, in the next week?**

TEXTS & TWEETS

When you get discouraged, where do you turn? What do you do? Come for some hope-filled insights.

Discover new ways to show kindness to the world around you. Join us this week, and bring along a friend!

Make texting your group easier. Consider using Simply Text. To try it FREE go to https://secure.symt.us/signup

THINGS TO REMEMBER

LESSON No.07

A ROYAL APPOINTMENT

BIBLE VERSES
Esther 4:1-17 Esther 9:20-22
Deuteronomy 31:6

ACTIVITY

Spend a few minutes discussing the news item or historical event.

Ask:

- **Why do we enjoy rooting for the "little guy" or the underdog? Why does the idea of one person making a huge difference capture our attention and imagination?**
- **When has one choice made a huge impact in your life, your family, or your community? Tell about it and why that one decision was so significant.**
- **Sometimes we talk about a person being "in the right place at the right time." Does that happen randomly or because of other reasons? Does this phrase discount God's role in opening doors and giving us opportunities? Why or why not?**

Say: **All these individuals had unique opportunities to affect history by their actions. Few of them knew ahead of time what the outcome of their actions would be, but they made their choices despite the considerable personal risk, and they sparked change. One person really can make a big difference.**

DIGGING IN

Have students take turns reading aloud Esther 4:1-17.

Say: **Let's look at Esther and the Jews to discover how we can be ready for the "royal appointments" God may bring into our lives.**

PURSUE COURAGE AND BOLDNESS

Say: **In the face of destruction, Esther chooses to take action to save her people, at the risk of her own life. When we trust in God, we'll find the courage we need to do what he asks of us.**

Ask:

- **Read Mordecai's words to Esther in verses 13-14. You may have**

Things you need...

- ☐ Bibles
- ☐ A news clipping (or video) that highlights a victory by an underdog. It can be about a sports team defeating its favored opponents or an attorney defending a whistleblower.

Consider examples from history:

- ☐ A protester in 1989 stood up against a tank in Tiananmen Square, in Beijing, China. This "little guy" put himself in harm's way to make a statement about human and political rights. (http://en.wikipedia.org/wiki/File:Tianasquare.jpg)
- ☐ Todd Beamer and other passengers on Flight 93 took on hijackers on September 11, 2001, to prevent further attacks on Washington, D.C. (http://en.wikipedia.org/wiki/Todd_Beamer)
- ☐ German manufacturer Oskar Schindler saved nearly 1,200 Jews during the Holocaust by giving them jobs in his factories. His story was made into the movie *Schindler's List*. (http://en.wikipedia.org/wiki/Oskar_Schindler)

BIBLE BACKGROUND

Read Esther 4:1-17.

Esther is a biblical Cinderella. A young woman who grew up in the care of her elder cousin, Mordecai, Esther is raised in a community of Jews who remain behind in Persia after their 70-year captivity ends. They stay to continue the successful lives and businesses they've started, but they're certainly religious and ethnic minorities among the people King Xerxes rules in the Persian Empire.

Esther becomes queen by a series of choices and seeming coincidences. Although God isn't mentioned directly in the whole account, Esther's story demonstrates God's continuing care for his people. By chapter 4, Esther has already been chosen as queen and is proving her loyalty to King Xerxes by exposing a plot against him. Jewish people continue to celebrate their rescue marked in the book of Esther with a holiday called Purim, or the Feast of Lots.

read or heard this before, especially the idea of Esther being queen "for just such a time as this." What does this tell you about Mordecai's faith in God? How are these words relevant to your life today?

- **As Esther thought about what she should do, what emotions do you think she experienced?**
- **When was the last time you faced a situation that required courage or boldness? Tell about the experience and how it impacted you. Were you able to act courageously because your fear went away? Why or why not?**

PRACTICE PRAYER AND FASTING

Ask:

- **Have you ever fasted before? If so, what was that experience like? If it challenged you spiritually, share how it did.**
- **Why might God want us to fast in certain situations? What does it accomplish?**
- **Throughout Scripture, we read about people praying and fasting. Jesus taught his disciples to pray and fast, too. What's the relationship between prayer and fasting?**
- **Jesus tells us to pray about the decisions we make, but if he already knows what's best for our lives, why does he want us to pray about our choices and actions?**

Say: **Once she knows the decision she has to make, Esther asks Mordecai and the Jews of her city to fast and pray with her before she goes to the king with her request. God gives us strength when we seek him. Fasting is a way of denying our everyday desires and focusing on our need for spiritual food—prayer, Scripture, worship, and service to others.**

TAKE TIME TO CELEBRATE AND SERVE

Say: **When you read ahead in Esther, you see in chapter 7 how Esther boldly exposes Haman's evil plot against the Jews. Haman is executed, and the Jews are saved. They celebrate what God has done for them by feasting and giving gifts of food to the poor. The Festival of Purim is marked by the dramatic reading of the entire book of Esther to remember and celebrate God's provision in their time of need.**

Ask:

- **Tell us about the best party or celebration you've ever attended. Why was it such fun?**
- **Cities celebrate after sports teams win championships. Families celebrate when a loved one returns home from the military.**

Couples celebrate the birth or adoption of a child. What are some great "excuses to celebrate" for Christians?

- In Esther 9:20-22, we see that the Jews didn't just celebrate; they also gave gifts of food to the poor. Why?

DIGGING DEEPER

Ask:

- Read Deuteronomy 31:6. If you adopted this as a defining verse or your "life motto," how would it influence your words and actions? What does it mean for God to "personally go ahead of you"?
- The story of Esther hinges on making the right decisions in the right circumstance to get to the next place God will move through her for his purposes—to protect his people. This journey of decisions involves risking herself for the greater good. In what way is Esther's decision a foreshadowing of Jesus' own selfless sacrifice to save us from sin's punishment? What similarities and differences do you see?
- The Jews of Esther's time and place lived in a diverse culture, but it's clear they had a strong identity as God's chosen people. What are some challenges you face maintaining and living out your Christian faith in our culture today?

PUTTING IT INTO PRACTICE

Ask:

- Esther was queen "for just such a time as this." When have you felt as though you are the "right person at the right time" to make a difference for Jesus?
- Esther shows her faith by her actions; she chooses to trust and obey God when facing difficult circumstances, even though she doesn't know exactly how her story will end. How does the story of Esther affect the way you think about your everyday circumstances and decisions—and your most difficult moments, too?
- Have you ever felt that the choices you make could change the world? Why or why not?
- Prayer is mentioned several times in Esther's story. What decisions or circumstances can you be praying about right now? How can we pray for each other?

Say: Consider taking a challenge to fast at some point this week.

TEXTS & TWEETS

Got the courage to step toward trouble in order to save others from it? Learn where the power for that comes from this week.

Need a little inspiration in your life? This true hero will give you some.

Maybe you want to fast from food for an entire day, or from TV, your phone, or music for the entire week. Whatever you choose to do, take the time you'd normally eat or participate in an activity and spend it in prayer and Bible reading. Keep a journal of what God teaches you during these times.

BONUS ACTIVITY

Follow the footsteps of the Jews after God's miraculous delivery. After Esther's pleas to the king spared the Jews, a new decree was sent, telling them to celebrate by feasting and sending gifts to the poor. As a group, collect donations of food for a local food bank and volunteer to help carry out its mission.

THINGS TO REMEMBER

LESSON No.08

ROOTED

BIBLE VERSES

Psalm 33
Proverbs 3:1-4, 13-26
Jeremiah 17:7-8
Colossians 2:6-7

ACTIVITY

Welcome students and open in prayer. Show the video clip.

Ask:

- **Many trees toppled over during Hurricane Sandy in 2012. Why do you think some trees fell but other similar trees remained standing?**
- **What things do you think contribute to healthy roots in a tree?**

Say: **Strong roots require not only good soil but also intentional care and maintenance along the way. As Christ-followers, we can be rooted in our faith by using the tools Jesus gives us in the Bible.**

Have someone read aloud Jeremiah 17:7-8.

Say: **Today we'll focus on what we can do to root ourselves deeper in the faith, helping us trust Jesus in every aspect of our lives.**

DIGGING IN

Have students take turns reading aloud Psalm 33.

Say: **Let's explore the poetic verses of this psalm and see what we can understand both about the psalmist and about God.**

READING THE BIBLE BUILDS YOUR TRUST IN GOD

Ask:

- **Why is the psalmist praising God in this psalm?**
- **In verse 4, the psalmist talks about the Word and trusting God. What are some areas of your life where you trust God, and where do you struggle to trust him?**
- **Share something from this psalm that makes you feel peaceful, and why.**

Say: **Psalm 33 reminds us of God's awesome strength and unfailing love. It reveals that God made everything and that all his plans are good and just.**

Things you need...

- ☐ Bibles
- ☐ A video clip of a tree being uprooted during a hurricane: http://tinyurl.com/jqjadp3 (Show the video from the 0:39 mark to the end.)
- ☐ An Internet connection and a computer or tablet to display the video

BIBLE BACKGROUND

Read Psalm 33.

In *Praying the Psalms*, Walter Brueggemann teaches about being securely oriented or well settled. When we're oriented, we understand what's right—that life makes sense and fits into what we know to be status quo. We're easily reminded of God's awesomeness and, through Scripture, imagine the Holy Spirit's love, beauty, power, and profound presence at work in our lives.

The writer of Psalm 33, who some believe to be David, praises God for who he is and how we are in relation to him. Note that the verses don't contain much revelation or speculation. The psalmist is simply giving God the credit due him, for his majesty and splendor.

Imagine God breathing life into his creation. Picture him uttering something into existence. The beautiful simplicity of that can be a reminder of God's abounding love for us and his creation. It reminds us to trust in God's wisdom, seek his protection, and recognize that he's always with us.

Reading and remembering Psalm 33 can equip teenagers to be rooted in who they are as Christ-followers. By remembering its truth, they can draw wisdom from it during affliction or adversity.

THE BIBLE OPENS YOUR EYES TO GOD'S POWER AND BEAUTY

Ask:

- **Where in this psalm does God reveal beauty?**
- **What is the psalmist celebrating in this psalm?**
- **God can speak something into existence—how does that compare to our own ability to create things?**

Say: **God is so powerful; he breathes the word and stars form. Because it's hard to imagine God's might, it can be so easy to forget the divine that's revealed to us every day. Think about the beauty of the sky, the ocean, the sun and moon, and the stars. Perhaps this psalm can help us remember some stuff we take for granted.**

KNOWING THE BIBLE MAKES YOU MORE SECURE IN YOUR FAITH

Ask:

- **How does this psalm help you feel secure in your relationship with Jesus?**
- **What do you think is the psalmist's point in verses 16 and 17?**
- **What does it mean to put hope in the Lord?**
- **How can the message of this psalm help you feel more rooted in your faith?**

Say: **By reading the Bible, we can grow in our faith by understanding the heart of Jesus and what it looks like to be in relationship with him. Psalm 33 reveals God's majesty and power and reminds us to trust in him and his unfailing love for us. How can the God who spoke the world into existence not be capable of handling anything we put in his care?**

DIGGING DEEPER

Ask:

- **Read Proverbs 3:1-4, 13-26. What do these verses say about the importance of wisdom?**
- **Can a person be wise without knowledge? Why or why not? What's the difference between knowledge and wisdom?**
- **What are some specific ways you have learned to know Jesus better?**

PUTTING IT INTO PRACTICE

Ask:

- **Being rooted in the Bible takes time and dedication. What things get in the way of knowing the Bible more fully? What has so far helped you overcome those obstacles?**

- **What are some insights you have about trusting Jesus? What are some ways you've learned to trust him more fully? This week, what's one thing you can hand over to Jesus?**
- **When you feel alone, what or who else—in addition to Jesus—can you turn to for comfort?**
- **Make a goal to read your Bible more often, and share your goal with someone. Ask that person to hold you accountable.**

THINGS TO REMEMBER

TEXTS & TWEETS

How is the message of the Bible making you stronger? Can't wait to hear your thoughts.

Are you rooted in Jesus? Come for some gardening—and faith—tips this week!

Make texting your group easier. Consider using Simply Text. To try it FREE go to https://secure.symt.us/signup

LESSON No.09

PAIN AND SUFFERING

BIBLE VERSES **Psalm 137** 1 Peter 5:8-10 John 16:33

ACTIVITY

Welcome students and open in prayer. Hand out the lyrics and play the song.

Ask:

- **What do you think this song is about?**
- **Think of a time you've felt as if you didn't have any strength left. What does this song say about where strength comes from?**

Say: **This song was inspired by a little girl who was dying from cancer. She loved Jesus and often asked her mom to read her Scripture to help her feel better. Casting Crowns knew of the family and received email updates on the girl's health status. Many times the mother had good news. Other times, she simply sent a prayer request because her daughter's condition had taken a bad turn. The mother shared her hope in Jesus, and she even admitted to praying while literally standing on her Bible. Even knowing her daughter was going to lose the fight with cancer, this mom found strength in God's Word.**

Ask:

- **Knowing a little bit about the story behind the song, what do you think the main message is?**
- **Why do you think the mother chose to stand on her Bible?**
- **When have you relied on Jesus and his Word during a difficult time?**

DIGGING IN

Have students take turns reading aloud Psalm 137.

Say: **Let's dig a little deeper to see if we can discover something new about ourselves and about Jesus.**

Things you need...

- ☐ Bibles
- ☐ Download the Casting Crowns song "Praise You in This Storm" (Track 2 on the *Lifesong* album).
- ☐ You'll need a way to play the song for students.
- ☐ Prepare handouts with the lyrics so students can follow along.
- ☐ Beforehand, read the background about why the song was written.

BIBLE BACKGROUND

Read Psalm 137.

Painful disorientation, as Walter Brueggemann explains in *Praying the Psalms*, is when we discover the reality of disorder or chaos. Things such as divorce, the death of a loved one, illness, or even a less serious challenge such as a fender bender, a failing grade, or the flu can cause disorientation—resulting in the sudden awareness that the world is dangerous and frightening. In fact, we don't have to look far to notice that many others (whether they're people we know or people we see on TV) are hurting or afraid.

Ultimately, the realization that we aren't alone in our laments can be the catalyst that sets us free to find hope and peace in waiting for what God has planned. One way we can be reminded of God's presence in our lives is by reading the Bible more. That way, when we encounter suffering, fear, or uncertain times, we're more likely to remember God in the first place.

WHEN LIFE IS HARD, YOU'RE NEVER ALONE

Ask:

- **What's your impression of the captives (the Israelites) and the captors (the Babylonians)?**
- **Why would the Israelites want to hang up their instruments?**
- **Where in this psalm can you feel the psalmist's pain? How can you relate better with the Bible passage by trying to envision yourself in the story?**
- **What does the psalmist say about not forgetting? Why do you think not forgetting Jerusalem was important?**
- **In these verses, what is the psalmist saying about God?**

Say: **This psalm reminds us that when we experience pain or have a problem, we're often not going through it alone. By reading about other people's painful experiences, we can more easily recognize that God was present then and be reminded that he's here now.**

LET GO AND PLACE YOUR TRUST IN GOD

Ask:

- **What does the psalmist ask God for? Why do you think he makes that request?**
- **What does that say about how the psalmist trusted God?**
- **What does it mean that the psalmist prayed to God for revenge instead of taking revenge for himself?**
- **When you're left to do nothing but wait, how does that impact your relationship with God?**
- **If God is the reason we overcome whatever trials or tribulations we're in, what's our role in helping others deal with their problems?**

Say: **The writer of this psalm is pretty angry about the terrible things that have happened to his people. But what's more interesting is that the psalmist doesn't try to take revenge on his captors. He leaves that up to God. He understands that God is in everything and relies on God's strength to pull him through. If we "let go and let God," then we also have to understand that we aren't God. And though we may have an easier time trusting God with our problems, what about trusting God with other people's problems? That's a big step for many of us.**

DIGGING DEEPER

Ask:

- **Read 1 Peter 5:8-10. What does this Bible passage tell us about** suffering? In addition to staying alert, what are other things we can do when we're in pain? How does the promise in these verses impact your hope?

- **Read John 16:33. What does Jesus say about trials and sorrows? What does it mean to have peace in Jesus Christ?**

PUTTING IT INTO PRACTICE

Ask:

- **When it comes to suffering, what are some healthy and good things you've done to deal with your pain?**
- **If you think about how Jesus responded to people who were suffering, how does that inform how you can respond to a friend who's suffering? Instead of trying to give advice or convince a person to try something else, what can we do to help another person who's experiencing challenges?**
- **Feeling pain is tough, and sometimes it's even harder seeing someone else feel pain. Is the trust we have in Jesus dependent on him doing what we hope he'll do, or dependent on something else? Explain.**

THINGS TO REMEMBER

TEXTS & TWEETS

Experiencing pain and suffering in life? Find healing among your friends, and bring one along.

How can we help others who are hurting or in pain? We'll talk about it this week.

Make texting your group easier. Consider using Simply Text. To try it FREE go to https://secure.symt.us/signup

LESSON No.10

IN THE VALLEY

BIBLE VERSES
Psalm 22
Jeremiah 29:11-13
Hebrews 2:18

ACTIVITY

Number off your teenagers by ones and twos. Then ask the twos to stand up and balance on one leg until you tell them to stop. Then go into your Intro and remind them to keep balancing on one leg until you finish talking.

Things you need...

- ☐ Bibles

DIGGING IN

Have students take turns reading aloud Psalm 22.

Say: **Life can feel easy when you're having mountaintop experiences. But when we're walking through the valleys, it can be excruciating. It can feel like standing on one leg, and not knowing when you'll be able to stop. And you see others around you who don't have to endure what you're going through, and it's easy to resent them or envy them or just give up hope. We all have bad days, but sometimes we experience an entire season of pain. We're desperate to be saved from the pit. Let's dig a little deeper into this psalm to see what Jesus reveals to us.** (Tell the kids balancing on one leg that they can sit down again.)

AT TIMES, LIFE SEEMS HOPELESS

Ask:

- **Why is abandonment one of the worst feelings or emotions we can experience?**
- **In verse 1, the psalmist asks God why he's abandoned him. When have you wondered the same thing?**
- **Explain the shift that happens in verse 3 when the psalmist uses the word "yet."**
- **The psalmist, though in absolute desolation, doesn't blame God but rather recognizes God's holiness. That doesn't seem to make sense—what's motivating that response, in your experience?**
- **In your own experience, why is it hard to trust Jesus when you're spending time "in the valley"?**

BIBLE BACKGROUND

Read Psalm 22.

The desert can be brutal, especially if we're spending lots of time there. A number of personal and family challenges can lead to a season in the valley. Other times, social issues such as war, an economy crash, or upheavals can also affect us. Regardless of the cause, when we're hurting we need to remember: (1) We aren't alone; (2) God has plans for us; and (3) through the adversity, God is strengthening us.

Facing unexpected catastrophes can be scary. We know God is with us in everything, but we're often impatient, forgetting that we don't understand God's timeframe or intentions. In the worst times, we may wonder if God is listening or if he cares that we're suffering. The bottom line is that God does care, he has a plan, and it's a good one.

Many theologians believe Psalm 22 is a foretelling of Christ's crucifixion a thousand years before it happened. Others believe David wrote it during a time of great duress. Regardless of the interpretation, the excruciating pain in the words is a potent reminder of what *did* happen on the cross. Jesus experienced time in the desert while suffering his crucifixion. Students will see that no matter what trial they face, they can *always* hope in God's power.

Say: **Psalm 22—whether viewed as the voice of King David himself or as the words and thoughts of Jesus prophesied—models how we often feel when we experience a major struggle or disappointment, disorienting us from what we know to be true. We all have experienced or will experience times of trial and tribulation when we feel hopeless and abandoned by God. Perhaps, though, we can model ourselves after the psalmist; instead of blaming God for our problems, we can have a "yet" moment—trusting God and his plans for us.**

JESUS BORE THE WORLD'S SINS TO REDEEM US

Ask:

- **Like Jesus, the psalmist writes about awful things being inflicted on him. What are some things in this psalm that are similar to Jesus' crucifixion?**
- **The psalmist speaks of God not answering his cries after days of pleading for help. Is that what's really happening, or is there some other explanation?**
- **What do you think it says about God that he's able to speak something into existence?**
- **In verses 12-21, the psalmist appears to be on the brink of death and begs for deliverance. Then something happens in verse 22. Explain what the psalmist is saying.**
- **What is significant about the vows the psalmist makes?**

Say: **God knows what it means to suffer. Jesus, God's Son, became a man, lived a human life, and was treated like a king in one instant and then as dirt in another. He willingly suffered the most heinous death so we may be reunited with him in heaven. Sometimes during our own suffering, it helps to remember that we haven't experienced anything that Jesus hasn't already experienced.**

WE CAN FIND HOPE IN PAIN

Ask:

- **Read Psalm 22 again. Despite the psalmist's pain, what messages of hope do you see in this Bible passage?**
- **At the beginning of the psalm, the psalmist pleads for God to take away his troubles. How does the prayer become bigger than just a cry for help?**
- **How did God use Jesus' suffering as a means to an end?**
- **Share a time when you suffered but were strengthened in the process. What did you learn from that experience?**

Say: **It isn't fun dealing with issues that cause us to feel pain, fear, or**

abandonment. But ultimately, God is turning our ugly into beauty as we give it to him. We know this because the Bible is full of messages that reiterate God's power and good intentions. Our hope—and our victory—is in Jesus.

DIGGING DEEPER

Ask:

- **Read Hebrews 2:18. What's one way Jesus helps us when we're experiencing pain?**
- **Read Jeremiah 29:11-13. What does this passage say about hope?**
- **What does it mean to seek Jesus wholeheartedly? How can we do that?**

PUTTING IT INTO PRACTICE

Ask:

- **Absolutely nothing is easy about suffering. Can you name some opportunities we have to grow when we experience challenging times?**
- **In what way does the psalmist pray to God? What would it look like for you to emulate the psalmist's approach to praying through pain?**
- **By reading Psalm 22, what have you discovered about waiting on God?**

THINGS TO REMEMBER

TEXTS & TWEETS

How can we find hope in pain? Share your ideas when our group meets.

Have you ever suffered and wondered where God was? Join us for some great discussions, and bring a friend, too.

Make texting your group easier. Consider using Simply Text. To try it FREE go to https://secure.symt.us/signup

LESSON No.11

TRUE STRENGTH

BIBLE VERSES
Psalm 13
Romans 5:1-6

ACTIVITY

Welcome students and open in prayer. Hand out the lyrics and play the song.

Ask:

- **How is this song similar to some of the psalms we've read and discussed?**
- **What promise does the song mention?**
- **What do you think the motivation behind this song is?**

Say: **Perhaps Phil Wickham recognizes that many people forget that God is always with them. Perhaps he's singing to everyone needing hope. One thing is clear, though: The singer reads his Bible, and he draws on that knowledge in order to share Jesus' hope with others.**

DIGGING IN

Have students take turns reading aloud Psalm 13.

Say: **Let's find out how we can more fully trust in God's power.**

WE CAN TRUST THAT GOD IS ALWAYS WITH US

Ask:

- **In Psalm 13, how can we tell that David still trusts God, even during his time of tribulation?**
- **What does David trust God to do for him, and why?**
- **What does David say will happen after he's restored, and how does he know it will happen?**

Say: **Though this is another psalm in which David pleads for God to bring him out of affliction, he never blames God for his predicament. He doesn't ask why God isn't helping him. David pleads with God to save him simply because he trusts that God is the only one who has the power to do that.**

Things you need...

- ☐ Bibles
- ☐ Download Phil Wickham's song "Safe" from the *Heaven and Earth* album.
- ☐ You'll need a way to play the song for students.
- ☐ Prepare handouts with the lyrics so students can follow along.

BIBLE BACKGROUND

Read Psalm 13.

Disorientation is an opportunity to learn and grow. When we're experiencing it firsthand, though, we don't always recognize God's presence in our lives. We may wonder what the point of all the suffering is. But if we learn from the psalms we've been studying, perhaps we'll see the deeper purpose of our pain. Instead of asking "why," we can ask "what." What does God have in store for me? What can I do to draw closer to God? What should I do to prepare for what God has in store?

Consider what many people intentionally put themselves through to physically grow stronger. Weightlifters strive for complete muscle fatigue. They understand that to grow stronger, they must shred their muscles. Pushing muscles to the point of fatigue breaks them down, which causes pain. But when the muscles regenerate, they knit themselves back together stronger than before.

This week's lesson will help students understand that they can trust God to always be present, that his plans are always good, and that out of the pain, they can emerge stronger than before.

PRAYER CAN BECOME A SOURCE OF STRENGTH

Ask:

- **What do all the psalms we've read and discussed so far have in common?**
- **Many of the psalms are simply prayers written out—based on what you've experienced in them so far, what's the purpose of these prayers?**
- **When you're facing a struggle or problem, how does it help when someone simply listens to you? In a similar way, when have you shared your situation with Jesus, and what happened as a result?**
- **Why is prayer an important part of our relationship with Jesus?**

Say: **Having a strong, conversational prayer life is just like having a strong, conversational relationship with a spouse or the people who are close to you. Communication strengthens relationship. And when you're used to talking about everything to that important person in your life, it's much easier to share the hard things that are going on. Prayer helps us "taste and see" that Jesus is always good.**

WE CAN GROW STRONGER BY EXPERIENCING HARDSHIP

Ask:

- **How does David expect to be better after being saved, and why?**
- **For whom will David be better?**
- **Looking back, how have you been strengthened through trial and tribulation?**
- **If Jesus is good and his plans for us are good, how do you see him working for our good during our trials and tribulations?**

Say: **Like weightlifters who shred their muscles in order to gain more strength, we'll be stronger for going through trials and tribulations. If we lean into Jesus during our hardships, we'll draw near to him and experience his heart in deeper ways than we've ever done before.**

DIGGING DEEPER

Ask:

- **Read Romans 5:1-6. Why does Paul say we have peace with God, and what does he mean by "peace"?**
- **Why does Paul urge us to rejoice when facing problems or trials?**
- **In times of darkness, what brings hope?**

PUTTING IT INTO PRACTICE

Ask:

- **When you're sharing with Jesus during tough times, what's** something physical you can do that communicates humility and openness while you're praying?

- One way to build toward a more everyday, conversational prayer life with Jesus is to simply make prayer the first thing you do when you get up in the morning and the last thing you do before you go to sleep. What are some other ideas that have helped you?
- Does "looking on the bright side of things" really make a difference? Why or why not? Instead, try something new—when you're struggling with something, just breathe this prayer over and over: "Jesus, have mercy on me."

THINGS TO REMEMBER

TEXTS & TWEETS

If working out hurts, why do people put themselves through it? Let's see how that connects to our faith in Jesus.

What can help us trust Jesus more? See you soon for some strengthening exercises!

Make texting your group easier. Consider using Simply Text. To try it FREE go to https://secure.symt.us/signup

LESSON No.12 GOD'S GRACE AND RENEWAL

BIBLE VERSES
Psalm 103 2 Corinthians 12:6-10
John 11:17-44

ACTIVITY

Turn off your meeting-room lights and have kids close their eyes and put both hands over their eyes, one over the other. It should feel like they're in a pitch-black room.

Ask:

- **What do you like about being in the dark, and what do you not like?**
- **Why do we use "darkness" as a metaphor for pain or struggle or confusion?**

Things you need...

☐ Bibles

DIGGING IN

Have students take turns reading aloud Psalm 103 (they might remember portions of this psalm from Lesson 3: "God Is Patient").

Say: **We've been discussing how life can be hard but how Jesus is working, like an artist, to bring beauty into our lives in the midst of tough times. He wants to fill us with hope in his power and vision for our life. Mainly we've been talking about how we can remember that Jesus is always with us, even though we may feel alone or abandoned. Today we'll consider how Jesus can renew us in surprising ways, especially when we're spending time "in the valley." Let's dive into what King David says in this psalm.**

GOD OFTEN SURPRISES US WITH A NEW PERSPECTIVE

Ask:

- **Tell about an area of your life where you've recently gained a fresh, new perspective. It doesn't have to be something overly spiritual—just something you're seeing from a different viewpoint. How did it happen, and what is it teaching you?**
- **Why is David praising God in this psalm?**
- **In verses 3-6, David uses the present tense when he describes God's deeds—why is that important?**

BIBLE BACKGROUND

Read Psalm 103.

In this lesson, students will see what happens when God pulls us through to the other side of the desert. We'll look at what author Walter Brueggemann calls *reorientation*, or our post-desert experiences. It's often evoked by a surprising gift of friendship and care, gestures of reconciliation and forgiveness, or signs of hope. In other words, we can emerge into reorientation due to experiences that touch us deeply and announce that God hasn't left the world in chaos after all.

Reorientation doesn't mean returning back to the way things were before life got tough. It's different from orientation because through our disorientation, we're given the opportunity to see God in a new way. We gain a broader perspective of God than we had before.

Many people believe David wrote Psalm 103 as an older man, reflecting on God's mercy and grace and urging all to praise God wholeheartedly. Reading Psalm 103 will help students see the surprising revelations David experienced after being delivered from affliction.

- **David had a difficult reign as king—including harmful choices he made and betrayal and rebellion from within his own family. How does that tough past show up here in his expressions of faith in God?**
- **How is David using his story to remind others that God deserves all the glory?**

Say: **Psalm 103 is like reading the personal journal of someone who's suffering a great deal, but still is able to remember God's goodness. Somehow, King David can be brutally honest about his circumstance but still be overcome with a thankful heart. David's joy is so great that he wants everyone to know of God's might and power.**

THROUGH HIS GRACE, GOD DELIVERS US FROM THE PIT

Ask:

- **Look at verses 8-13. What are some ways God gifts us with his grace?**
- **If it weren't for God's grace or power, how would things be different for us when we experience times of trial?**
- **David says God does this for us because he knows we're only dust. What does he mean when he uses that metaphor?**

Say: **God doesn't just have a vision for our lives; he is working in partnership with us to bring that vision into reality. Our problem is that many times, especially when we're struggling, we forget that he is faithful to do what he's said he'll do. It's natural to get impatient and forget that God is constantly molding us and refining us. He's the only one who saves us, and he does it for real—it's not just words with him.**

GOD'S POWER CAN HEAL AND RENEW US

Ask:

- **In the first two verses, David summons everything that he is—some translations refer to the soul—to praise the Lord. If past experiences lend to who a person is, what is David saying here?**
- **In verses 3-5, what leads to David being redeemed?**
- **How does David explain the way God renews us?**

Say: **David begins this psalm by praising God with everything he is. This means he's recalling everything—good and bad—that has made him the man he is. And he praises God for it all. On the other side of his suffering, David realizes that God's heart is good, and that he's working for good in his life. Even if it hurts in the process, David is better for it in the end.**

DIGGING DEEPER

Ask:

- **Read John 11:17-44. Jesus uses his power to call Lazarus out of the tomb, even though it's been four days since his death. What's most surprising in this account, and why? What are all the ways Jesus uses his power to heal and renew? Look for both the obvious and non-obvious...**
- **Read 2 Corinthians 12:6-10. Paul speaks about not boasting because he doesn't want to describe himself in ways people haven't actually experienced him. He doesn't want to "pad his resume," so to speak. So Paul is given a "thorn in his flesh"—he calls it a "messenger from Satan"—that's designed to keep him from "becoming proud." Why does Jesus respond to Paul the way he does? And why does that make Paul want to "boast" about his weaknesses?**
- **When have you been reminded that Jesus makes you strong in the midst of your weaknesses?**

PUTTING IT INTO PRACTICE

Ask:

- **We don't always recognize Jesus' grace when it comes to us, and we don't always respond to it when we do. What's a simple phrase you can say softly to Jesus whenever you sense his grace in your everyday life?**
- **What phrase can you tell yourself to remember Jesus' grace whenever you're facing struggles?**

THINGS TO REMEMBER

TEXTS & TWEETS

Where have you felt Jesus' grace in your life? Join us, and share your story.

When have you been surprised by Jesus' vision for your life? We'd love to hear your story.

Make texting your group easier. Consider using Simply Text. To try it FREE go to https://secure.symt.us/signup

13 ESSENTIAL LESSONS FROM THE OLD TESTAMENT

LESSON

REAL POWER

No.13

BIBLE VERSES

Psalm 30
Daniel 2:21-22
1 Corinthians 2:1-5
Philippians 2:12-13

DIGGING IN

Have students take turns reading aloud Psalm 30.

Say: **Most people are inclined to take credit when things are going well. But it's good to remember that Jesus is the one who strengthens us, and when he moves through us to make a good impact in someone's life, it's an opportunity for us to worship. Let's dive in and find out more about Jesus' power.**

1. REMEMBER JESUS' POWER AND STRENGTH

Ask:

- **In this psalm and the other psalms we've read, what sentence would the writers use to update their Facebook status?**
- **Why is David thanking God?**
- **We know Jesus is powerful, but we don't always see his power exercised when and where we want it—how does that impact your trust in him when you're in trouble?**
- **In verses 6 and 7, it sounds as if David got a bit too sure of himself. Whether God turned from him or not, David suffered. What are some things David remembers about God in the midst of his trial?**
- **What are some words that describe how David prays? What are some words that describe what he does after he's restored to health?**

Say: **King David was on top of the world. He even credits God for blessing him and making him prosperous. But then David gets overconfident in his own plans and goes against God's wishes by having the people of Israel numbered. Numbering was reserved for God alone. And because the Israelites freely participate in the numbering, God punishes them by making David choose one of three punishments. David chooses three days of sickness that end up killing 77,000 people. What a horrible outcome of his disobedience. It's easy**

Things you need...

- ☐ Bibles

BIBLE BACKGROUND

Read Psalm 30.

Reorientation can be caused by a gift of friendship, hope, and forgiveness. But sometimes, God simply steps in and reveals himself to us in undeniable ways. When that happens, we can't ignore God's supreme power.

Often, though, God uses us to pull other people from their despair. When that happens, it's easy to give credit to another, rather than God. Even the people God uses often take credit for themselves. Sometimes our motivation needs a check. Why do we do mission work or serve the poor, for example? Too often, it's because it makes us feel good. We feel powerful because of our own ability to affect others in a positive way. But we need to remember that God is working through us. He strengthens us to be his instruments.

In this lesson, students will consider how being reoriented in God gives them a story to share with others. Our story can be one of hope for people who may be in the desert. But ultimately, if God chooses to use us to help another out of the pit, he deserves the praise. In our weakness, he is strong. We can tell his story because we see his heart, exemplified by Jesus.

to forget that there are consequences—both large and small—when we go our own way instead of honoring what God has told us to do.

DON'T NEGLECT JESUS' POWER AND STRENGTH

Ask:

- **What does God say about his anger?**
- **What does God say about his favor? What do you think favor means?**
- **God's power can be scary. How is it a good thing to be afraid of God's power?**

Say: **Fear isn't always a bad thing. In fact, it's a natural emotional response that alerts us to danger, helping us avoid harm. Jesus' power is incredible and can be scary to behold. But fear may very well get us to stop, pay attention, and move in a new direction. Jesus' strength is great, but so is his mercy.**

JESUS' POWER AND STRENGTH TRANSFORM LIVES

Ask:

- **In what ways does God transform David?**
- **How do you think David is made stronger through his suffering?**
- **What's the significance of David's vows at the end of this psalm?**
- **How do you think God uses David's suffering for good in the long run?**

Say: **Many of the psalms detail how God uses his power and strength to renew and redeem. But plenty of passages in the New Testament also demonstrate how God can transform lives. No other story is more powerful than Jesus' resurrection. Always remember that it's through grace and by faith that Jesus promises to make us new again, whether in life or death. As followers of Jesus, we can be patient, study his Word, get to know his heart more deeply, and live a life of joy, even when we're facing affliction.**

DIGGING DEEPER

Ask:

- **Read 1 Corinthians 2:1-5. Pay attention to the way Paul describes his relational approach to the Corinthians—why is it significant?**
- **What does it mean to rely on "the power of the Holy Spirit" when we talk to others about Jesus?**
- **Read Daniel 2:21-22. What does this passage reveal about God's power? What does it tell us about wise and knowledgeable people?**

- **Read Philippians 2:12-13. Why would Paul give these instructions to the Philippians?**

PUTTING IT INTO PRACTICE

Ask:

- **How would others know that Jesus is at work in your life—what do you do or say that helps them see that?**
- **Jesus' power is bigger than anything—how do you know this is true, based on your own life?**
- **Using the topic index or concordance in your Bible, or by searching an online Bible resource like biblegateway.com, search for the words "strength" and "power" in the New Testament. What do you learn?**

THINGS TO REMEMBER

TEXTS & TWEETS

Why do you love helping others? We'd love to learn from you.

How has Jesus moved through you to help another person in trouble? See you soon for a great discussion.

Make texting your group easier. Consider using Simply Text. To try it FREE go to https://secure.symt.us/signup

13 ESSENTIAL LESSONS FROM THE NEW TESTAMENT

If you liked doing these lessons from the Old Testament, then you'll love the next in the series. Available online and at your local Christian bookstore.

ISBN 978-1-4707-4451-9